I0879352

Whiteout

Books by George Murray

Glimpse
The Rush to Here
The Hunter
The Cottage Builder's Letter
Carousel

George Murray

Whiteout

Poems

MISFIT

ecw press

Get the eBook free!

Purchase the print edition and receive the eBook free!
For details, go to www.ecwpress.com/eBook.

copyright © George Murray, 2012

Published by ECW Press
2120 Queen Street East, Suite 200, Toronto, Ontario, Canada M4E 1E2
416-694-3348 / info@ecwpress.com

All rights reserved. No part of this publication may be reproduced, stored in a retrieval system, or transmitted in any form by any process — electronic, mechanical, photocopying, recording, or otherwise — without the prior written permission of the copyright owners and ECW Press. The scanning, uploading, and distribution of this book via the Internet or via any other means without the permission of the publisher is illegal and punishable by law. Please purchase only authorized electronic editions, and do not participate in or encourage electronic piracy of copyrighted materials. Your support of the author's rights is appreciated.

Library and Archives Canada Cataloguing in Publication

Murray, George, 1971-
Whiteout / George Murray.
I. Title.
PS8576.U6814W45 2012 C811'.6 C2011-906944-X
ISBN: 978-1-77041-087-9
also issued as:
978-1-77090-235-0 (PDF); 978-1-77090-236-7 (EPUB)

Editor: Michael Holmes / a misFit book
Cover design: David Gee
Type: Rachel Ironstone
Printing: Coach House Printing 5 4 3 2

The publication of *Whiteout* has been generously supported by the Canada Council for the Arts which last year invested $20.1 million in writing and publishing throughout Canada, and by the Ontario Arts Council, an agency of the Government of Ontario. We also acknowledge the financial support of the Government of Canada through the Canada Book Fund for our publishing activities, and the contribution of the Government of Ontario through the Ontario Book Publishing Tax Credit. The marketing of this book was made possible with the support of the Ontario Media Development Corporation.

Canada Council for the Arts Conseil des Arts du Canada Canada ONTARIO ARTS COUNCIL CONSEIL DES ARTS DE L'ONTARIO

Printed and bound in Canada

Contents

Dante's Shepherd

(Inferno, Canto XXIV, Lines 1–15 Revisited)

At dawn I walk to the bank in the rain,
hood-peak pinned with one blue hand and wrist
forced from its sleeve (while its twin does not deign

to ditch the cuff, but hides instead, a fist
worrying, a clenching/unclenching tide,
mulling its wish to progress and subsist).

The sky clears itself while I am inside,
scuttling the dull clouds of a coastal morning
for white litter on blue with sun cockeyed.

It leans down on the hills as though scorning
any doubt that the universe still lives
without my happiness in bloom, warning,

Look down at those matching hands: where one thrives,
flush with life, if stiff and warming, the other,
also red and aching, only now arrives.

The New Weather

Just before the key catches in the lock
a snowflake lands on your eyelash and blurs
the scene; stretching the instant an instant
longer, slurring outer and inner worlds.

A moment, a moment more; you dare not
move, and so pause on the sill, wait for the tear
that will form in either the new weather
hot from the house, or your eye's open stare.

The Uncountable

Existence gets structured by measures set
against the innumerable, yet water
cupped in your hands remains as much the sea
as what rolls in at your feet.

Paper, sand, fruit, space, damage, milk, broken
down for the sake of each new telling;
sheets, grains, bushels, cubic feet, dollars, cups,
expression's separation.

Mass exists, numbers exist, but there's no
power one has over the other without
the intrusion of our invention;
piecemeal need for discretion.

Music, advice, electricity, blood,
data, news, sugar, furniture, cancer,
fire, mathematics, traffic, air; all
limited by discussion.

Love too is countless, but less inclined to be discrete.

Hundredth Monkey Effect

First peeling potatoes, then spinning jenny,
then suspension bridges, then dodging relapse;
insight works in hand-me-downs, rules of thumb.

Lives go by as one man leaves his plenty
to another, the gap jumped in one synapse
supplies a map, which becomes a custom.

If one went from few to all, skipping many,
or passing through it fast enough to perhaps
go unnoticed, that moment when some

have not yet been taught or given any
key for wisdom might not move in time-lapse,
might not leave memory's pool un-plumbed.

Signals could flit, antenna to antennae,
acumen inherited; not just the facts,
but the whole practice of giving come undone.

Would that we could just leave a penny
in payment for each other's thoughts, and collapse
the process of knowing to a simple sum.

New York

The man with all those balloon strings in hand
is a reverse marionette, compelling
the sky to lope like a yapping dog through the park.

To have emigrated so far only
to practice your crazy here among the games
and lights of the day's midway is like

a child tugging at a loose tooth and coming
away with the sturdy one beside it.
Our part of Earth tilts to the sun, a camper

turning her back to the flame to warm what
had been left too long in the dark cold.
The sky was a perfect tuxedo blue today,

and now my body is naked in the bed's heat,
each finger spread to allow for maximum
air current. Below the window,

the rats' bourbon in the bottom of the trash
climbs, a burglar on the brickwork's trellis.
The dead, you know better than most, do not

loop into themselves, but roll into us,
uploaded memories and ideas
of being, having been, burning up regret.

Do you remember how we held each other

despite the space between us? Each moment
hatched out of the last, genetically sad.

Gunshots blocks-away flash past, sound meteors,
there and gone instantly, with no evidence
of travel, but a good bit where they end up.

Even here we are on that planet,
subject to the same laws of heat's exchange
and air's resistance. It's why fast things light up.

Brushfires
(February 2009)

There are always bodies to discover
at each new disaster, in a range of states,
from seeming sleep to a charred disorder.

But once the inspections begin in earnest,
expect this death count to escalate
as the scorched landscape is closely assessed,

teeth and DNA separated, filed
as discrete, razed histories, aggregates
of last moments and final acts, the wild

fires closing in, their inverse-shadows
cast by a speeding sackcloth sun; innate
desire to touch, like first love, pupils aglow.

It's common enough to come across pairs
of bodies, dumped freight washed up in the surf,
broken on the pavement beneath barely

there buildings, or even camouflaged
in the charcoal and atomized silicate
of a brushfire, but harder to tell which vague

strewn ember was once man or woman,
or which was both; entwined in conjugate
burning, the heat put to use and flames fanned.

Falling or burning, embraced against the end;
what-was-once-two closes in, supplicates,
smoulders down to one corpse, crumbles, ascends.

A Race Around the Sun

In the car she tells you and the view opens
from the track you were speeding down to exposed
planes into which you whirl without direction.

In the rearview's periphery a year goes
by faster than it does through the windshield's wide
glimpse where cardinals spread and hurtle by close.

The disk on which these planets spin provides
at least lanes within lanes as definite tracks
down which falling appears as a forward ride.

Running out of road was a moment's heart attack
struck from life lived in a line, one designed to draw
the void back to the groove of parallax.

Turn the radio on and set your jaw
against all bearings and note instead the sound
the needle makes when dropped on the vinyl's flawed

circle, that scratched sky you've just gone around.

Saint Teresa of Ávila

If a caveman saw a movement in the night
and mistook it for another man,
he lost nothing but heart; but if a caveman
saw another man moving in the moonlight
and mistook if for nothing, he lost all.

So the crackling leaves become whispers,
bumps in rock the leering face, glint of moon
eyes staring, the flies and breeze fingers strewn
over the throat. Each night the same, from Vespers
to Morning Prayer; beware, or lose it all.

How to not lose it in your head's castle
when even the mere arrangement of stones sends
faces ghosting from the mason's accident,
troglodytes and lovers from life's sin and bustle?
Dream up saviours empty enough to fall through you.

And then we come to your golden spear,
Teresa, the point of which is lost in patterns
books made in your mind. Cutter or slattern,
saints comforted you, and angels, my dear,
thrust their weapons and caveman-selves through you.

Fuse

Between every two people runs a fuse,
a line from head to heart or heart to crotch,
cunt to mouth, eye to navel, hand to throat;
short or long, strung this way or that, welding

one desire to another love, one need
to another want, hate to deeper hate,
fear to loyalty, tremble to light touch,
flame to a bucket, fall to a turned back.

What's unique isn't its length or course,
whether travelling from one side or both,
or even who's stood at either end,
but ignition: just how and when it got lit.

Cowboy Story

The books sit on the shelf, a row of coma patients
in a ward, a series of selves no longer able to learn
and trapped at the point of injury: the last page.

At the donor clinic I offer my arm to the spigot
of the needle and think, as I see the bag fill
with blood, *there goes some of me*. But that's a lie:

as soon as it exits, the fluid is its own object,
with all the attendant foreignness and filthy infection
that implies, and has no meaning in terms of *me*.

Life happens like a cowboy story in which two
lines of gun-wielding men walk slowly toward each
other, skinning those smokewagons until the sky is white

with exploded gun powder. Out in the open, shooting
past all logic, they advance until either reality is killed
or they fall. I'm not saying there's no control,

but rather that control is all there is. Keep reading
to find out how it ends. The only cover offered is
the bad aim of enemies, and an adherence to the script.

The Accident

Time doesn't slip away like nameless traffic
accelerating from a red light.
It piles up, cars in a highway accident,

each slipping under the bumper of the next /
last on impact. If you're used to seeing
life as a line, it's easy to think the years

tick by when they're really just stacked up
above you. There's the changing lights, yellow signs
noted without memory, and there's the—

front end suddenly gone, other car
spun into oncoming lanes, doors opened,
dizzy exits, hands on trunks, a baby

rescued from his clamshell, head held, crying
surprise, crying rebirth. Old man,
young men, each slipped under the last,

look both ways for red lights and bystanders,
sirens approaching, emergency response.
Where were we? Time has already passed

this accident by, slowing itself, rubber-
necking, then continuing on its way.

The Snails

1.

And the rain keeps the sidewalk dark this morning,
an inverse Red Sea, water parting the desert
you walk to work—your mind engaged ticking
off obligations. And if you could picture

the last two hours of struggle as one minute,
a line of snails would burst from the green verge
like a salute of mistimed starters' bullets,
loping into leads and losses for the curb—

each corkscrew staircase shell a leaning sail
in a yacht race—the wind tilting this miniature
Exodus as it aims at an invisible
Promised Land. And some imperative Nature

has yet to explain to us draws them over
the concrete path we haven't yet explained to Her—
bodies scoured on the drying foundation,
eyestalks strained at some strange salvation.

2.

Sleep's void gives way to a quality of light
that yields to the dawn's sense of duty—
and night cedes to day without space to admit
what's been lost in both time and beauty.

Fingers count in pockets—two thirds of life
pledged to sleep and slow minds—and I predict
what promise remains will fail, humbled by lies
and cheques, both of which have become my product.

I fear I was mistaken, that I misspoke,
misheard, was unaware of the complex
nature of the situation—I leapt and broke,
before I looked, just what did not need fixed.

Habit and a path lead my morning walk,
and each hour that I tap on the stone of this clock
keeps water flowing and the Egyptians at bay,
but still leads to Jordan's bank as ordained.

3.

And amidst this well-composed painting of speed
sit odd wrecks, fragmented spirals cutting
through wet bodies—smashed chariots in a sea
of reeds—broken, not drowned. And it's not cunning

or God that saved some over others, but chance—
the feet of those keen or restless few
on their way to work ahead of you advanced
despite the slow story playing below.

And whether they did or didn't care,
and whether following under orders
or fleeing under orders, and whether
some even enjoyed the slight pop of life under

foot, you can't know. You're moving through the race
as one does a book, at a historian's pace—
wondering how, between catastrophic fate
and divine interest, life ever lasts the day.

Song for Memory

The old men are proud of their jukebox picks,
Humming in time where the words come unfixed,
Just five kings left, only four can turn tricks,
The tallow burns down to a bath for the wicks.

Some get it right while some make mistakes,
Some hear the chorus, some just the break,
Some mouth the verse through sips that they take,
Some rub their chins like their memories ache.

The harbour's socked in, the lighthouse is on,
And row upon row of the people they know
Stand still as a choir with the audience gone.

A full house is five men, but very few glances,
They shuffle the cards and hand out the chances,
Eye all the queens while the clock still advances,
And ponder their time in long empty trances.

Stuck in the space where their reach meets the view,
Where last thoughts hold on, but the first are too few,
They crackle like fire on its way up the flue,
Give what's deserving its day and its due.

The hands keep turning to follow the dawn,
And row upon row of the people they know
Stand still as a choir with the audience gone.

The fog has blown off, but still hangs in the lung,
A guitar's in the corner, its neck left unstrung,
The girl at the bar is impossibly young,
But the brass gets its wipe, and the pints still get slung.

No head goes unnodded, no head goes unhung,
The time to go home has long ago come,
The song goes around on its black vinyl tongue,
And row upon row of the people they know
Stand still as a choir that hasn't yet sung.
Stand still as a choir that hasn't yet sung.

Hung for a Sheep as a Lamb

Even with the brass ring in a bull's nose,
Paris knew the score—Go big or go home.
Birth each instant, a torch from your hole,

suck life down like milk from a bear's tit,
send a dog's limp tongue back as your death
medal—make your enemies scream it.

Some stunted thought begs me to tone it down,
nags over appearances—asks an ounce
of quiet, whispers from unplugged headphones.

What can we ask of this moment together
except others, better or worse?—more us, rather
than ambition's bit nail, or stillness and leisure.

First left for dead—next, heaven blessed.
Lovers can be fighters, but then best
at neither, when even wars start by kindness.

Take all you can carry, dear—all that I am.
Just as well hung for a sheep as a lamb.

St. John's

The rooftops' stammered Morse code, dot-dashing.
Inside it's pews and chairs. Closer down,
nail crowns crater in hardwood floorboards,
satellite imagery of all our hung heads.

Hibachi outside the corner store strip joint.
Today's drunk steady at it, as opposed
to yesterday's spectacular fellow.
Foam rises in the glass, the beer's prayer

to be more than it is, to overflow
itself, flesh from the tops of jeans, chatter
among the locals. Fat people roll down
gangplanks and point, the fog lifts on occasion,

the sewer's end posing for pictures.
Oiled pigeons hold off dry gulls, anoint
the sidewalk again and again. Storefronts close
around the club, girls pacing outside.

Your future could lean in that door and you
might not recognize it as anything
but the next in another series of nows.
They stand on the walk, many highway billboards

read as one: distinct markets, general moods.
On the ocean, waves exchange momentum,

wait their chance to go rogue. Somewhere under
every inch of skin is a Venn diagram

with lovers overlapping just so,
and it's here I want us to be. No one asked,
What if there's only the one universe?
If it turns out there is, then one is enough.

Pareidolia

The couple in the basement argue in the space
they've rented and we can hear every word:
shouted, spoken, or hissed through bitten lips.

From the patterns of paisleys on the wallpaper
faces emerge, grotesque little Mandelbrots that
once viewed cannot be unseen.

Constellations break into asterisms and form
bodies, flatbreads show saviours,
windows reflect a variety of virgins.

We sit quietly, hoping and dreading the fight
will finish before they reach and resolve
some issue of our own, saving us the trouble.

Makes me wonder what the people upstairs
think of these silent evenings at our desks,
and if those below hear aught from those below them.

Emergency Broadcast System

This is only a test. At the long tone
we will begin. At the long tone we will end.
At the long tone it is time for the news.
At the long tone you may begin to write.
When the bell rings you may rise to leave.
When the bells ring you may choose to flee.
The strike of the clock marks another birth.
The strike of the clock leaves welts shaped like hands.
Striking the clock marks another morning.
As the short tone sounds events will unfold.
As the short tone sounds the time will be right.
At the bell you will begin to salivate.
The experiment will begin when the toll
reaches all ears. The experiment will
begin when the topless lady wrings out
the last of her clothes. The experiment
involves pealing and will be double blind.
There are two strips of cloth for each ding you hear.
Please put them on, then record and report.
Ignore the mewl of the cat in the box.
The mewl of the cat in the box has no
relevance. Whether alive or dead
at the end of the experiment, you
must ignore all complaints from the cat.
Your first responsibility is to
the sound of the tone. Forget the cat.
Focus instead on the topless lady.
You have been provided with paper for notes.
You must take only the notes that are sung
to you. If you cannot hear the notes, you
may be shocked by the provided visuals.
The visuals will provide some context,

but will be shocking for some audiences.
The boom of the howitzer may make you jump.
The boom of the howitzer will connote
importance. The silver trumpets' peal will
announce a king arriving or leaving.
The chime will call you in for tea and cake.
The chime is pleasant, but cannot be ignored.
As the chime sounds, birds will fall dead from the trees.
The chime will signal your imminent passing
from one bicycle lane to the next.
The klaxon will sound loudly in warning.
The klaxon also cannot be ignored.
The klaxon will note the start of the baggage
carousel. The horn will give you the fright
of your life. The ringing of metal means
swords have been drawn. The ringing of metal
can never be good. The trolley's clang
might remind you of something fond and sweet.
The trolley's clang might remind you of your
forgotten suitcase. The whistle of the train
means all are aboard and accounted for.
The whistle of the train used to be
in the distance. The whistle of the train
now comes with a bright light. At the long tone,
the experiment is set to begin.
At the long tone you may begin to run.
Each pulse of your blood will count for one beat.
Each beat of your blood will be considered
a long tone. For today's purposes,
each pulse of your blood will be a starter
pistol in the distance, through water,
and echoed. Remember, this is only a test.

Owed

My debts are my blessings, so I stay home
to count what I haven't, and add no more.

The pots above the stove hang and ring
their slight touches as I enter the room.

Here are the facts of you alone, they sing.

The kitchen table is an accountant's desk.
Sit down without a plate, it says, among

the strewn toys and echoed noise of small wrecks.

Calculate not what's owed and owned,
but what's outstanding, and who that's for.

Ligature (fi)

You worked through your margins and I noted the mark,
so my character changed in the context of you
from a *just me* to something resembling an *us*.

Our bodies had already been glyphed when my mind
took its single *i*, spooned and subsumed by your *f*,
found those points at which touch and thought began to fuse.

Then we were reversed, despite our preferred arrays,
and left, turned into an *if*, without ligature
guiding our transition from *one* back to *a one*.

Yes, we are the type that must face doing the work
of two letters but, at least in what we've both just
written, we've had this chance to see ourselves as one.

Child's Play

Carefully. Carefully, another year
set down on this crooked stack of baby's blocks,
those at the top purposely off kilter
offset those below gone askew by mistake.

Only physics holds this up, the shared weight
each new addition loans to those below,
not x down for y above, just straight
friction, balance, leverage, sheer stress tau.

It began with one, two, three, but abruptly
nears forty, a wobbling tower. My aim
at setting has improved dramatically
since I began, but the bricks are still the same.

All These Waves

1.

The day would be hot if it weren't for the air,
the icebergs offshore radiating
a fog thick enough to obscure the docks—
the bright side of town's confused grey sister.

I need some perspective here, and not on
the view—a stance outside my pride and place,
an angle on obligation more oblique
than this established ethic might allow.

But there are different definitions
of clarity—in a nautical town
you needn't see the sun to be considered
clear, only the treeless horizon.

Instinct tells me to run from this circumstance,
but instinct is not thought—it's closer
to bone and muscle than revelation—
not dear to my heart, but dear to my need.

2.

It’s always a late spring by the ocean—
what you’re engaged in here is wilful mishearing,
mistakes that benefit understanding,
a baby’s cry in contrast to communal sense.

And you do the best with what you’ve heard, move
your lips, mimic as closely as possible—
hope others mishear the same way,
or differently enough to let you know.

Maybe you’ve misunderstood, maybe you
were wrong, maybe you were never meant to
head this roundabout way, maybe, maybe, may—
you just can’t tell with all these options.

What connections do form come like winter
deadfall—sticks strewn across one another
on the forest floor, nature’s poorly engineered
raft that is also its most fortunate art.

3.

The cool air on my tongue offers only
one sky's taste at a time, or perhaps
many blues' tastes stirred together to one—
easing this gourmand need for category.

I have no way to file this experience,
no sure slot to drop it in—in part
because I remain unsure enough of the whole
to doubt the truth of any component parts.

In the past, there were many options
for what I might see on the horizon—trees,
towers, buildings, the smog of choked cities—
but from here, all these waves make just one sea.

When you're backed into a corner, you can
always try to climb—when you run out
of land, you can swim out to the shaky boat—
other than that, you must remain completely still.

Blazon for the Crone

For a skeleton there is a spinning wheel over which she is pulled;
for a heart there is a bucket, a well, a rope—

Her mind, a covered bridge, lets each memory rattle
its loose planks, grow in the corners like spiderwebs—

She is older than either paint or harebell, lime-ancient:
tuskless, yet still able to paw sand in anticipation—

Invisible inside, there is a curved retina, a fingertip's blunt
nerve ending, an eardrum pulled tight as embroidery—

Outside, her world is a tongue with tastebuds numerous as
strawberry seeds
through which she moves, a glacier of salt.

Belfast

Pour me a bit of something to drink, and leave
it sitting on the counter until I get home—
I've got your pictures here to look at when
forgetting we're happy, for when the bonfires

light the underside of the clouds, when old
ladies yell into the phones their children
insisted they have, when the whiskey bonder
becomes the spirit merchant becomes the barman.

Served and reserved, I'm getten—move on down
the line. Crane-works unwinding, lifting
mostly air these days. They all look you straight
in the ear, past the shoulder's escape route.

Nobody's really here anymore, are they?
Friday nights empty of recognition,
except where women are helped home, fags lit,
barefoot, sandals dangling from a finger.

Ashes on TV, the river buried
below, a pipe under all neighbourhoods—
water's tangled hair straightened with a comb
into Brylcreemed rows of marching men.

Buses between streets, the population on
permanent inhale—short sucks of heaven

accumulate in the lungs, overcrowded
prisons, or each breath the clock needs for a tick.

Spare a moment for the buried mothers,
even if you're not the crying kind—
there's all this anger pointed at nothing,
a day's bad mood carried into the blood.

The Waiting Room

The doctors and nurses move in time-lapse
footage of clouds, but the room remains unchanged
despite shifts in wallpaper and sea foam paint—
scattered chairs, the uniform drip of taps.

Toys, watercolours, notice of change in fees,
magazines with retouched models' stares,
the remains of last summer's current affairs—
there is no answer in any of these.

Being here is change-neutral, as amongst
the dead, one point through which all those forced
wait to cease—Limbo's boat without momentum's oars,
but plenty of *here* to lean back against.

Song for a Divorce Budget

Two halfs don't always make a whole,
One can't always be split.
Three's not really good company,
Two can't tango worth shit.

Four is just not that fantastic,
Three can't pin down its roots.
Five's no longer so furious,
Four looks awful in suits.

Six is no beast when all alone,
Five does not a party make.
Seven ain't so lucky in love,
Six has no dice to shake.

Eight will never know it's enough,
Seven can't wait all week.
Nine won't dress to below the hilt,
Eight's not completely unique.

Ten can't live without decadence,
Nine won't be gauged in lives.
One ignores all lonesome numbers,
Zero loathes those who divide.

The World Goes Out Like an Old Television

It's nothing so sudden as power loss—
you've turned this set off each night for years,
the picture always returns in the morning.

No, it's something subtler, more natural,
a darkening under the skin—one night
the blue shudders a moment then returns,

another night the vertical goes,
the image getting up as though to leave.
And you just change the channel thinking

it must be the station's fault, or you slap
the side of the box with a slipper
and when everything returns you dismiss

the possibility of coincidence
and think yourself quite the mechanic.
Then every night for a year you hit that thing

until finally the blue goes completely—
then the yellow-green, until it's all some
bloody colour between red and black.

But by then your eyes, having grown accustomed,
can still see the image, and your ass,
so comfortable in the chair, doesn't feel

the need to move so long as your foot
can kick out—and even during the well-lit days
you're forever too busy with other

distractions to get it fixed. And so
when evening comes again you fool yourself
into thinking it's good for a day more—

and on that final quiet afternoon
you didn't know had arrived, in the middle
of your favourite show, when the picture shrinks

slowly to a bright dot, you aren't aware,
because, squinting, you can still make out the shapes—
and even as the lights recedes totally,

infinity and zero meet, saving you
from ever noticing a thing. And when
everything finally goes black, you sit

still, waiting in the dark for such a long time.

The Address Book

The days of address book updates are done;
copying from smudged and scored old entries
to empty sheets, trying to clarify

new acquaintances, and pin the drifting ones;
rewriting each name to record the days seized,
the admirable *fuck-its*, and long goodbyes

of those trading streets, cities, and countries;
one, three, six moves a year, gone. Now it's sure bets
and kids, homes and steady bucks, fine routine;

all those get-up-and-gos, those careless braveries,
dwindling over time to got-up-and-wents.
And the new turn up fewer and further between.

The Definition of Zero

The origin of any measurement;
value linking positive and negative;
completely obscured; the lowest point;
gone, not done; that which no longer lives.

cross section of an empty egg; gun sight;
cardinal; gravity; digit; freezing;
clear; even, oddly; wholly precise in time;
absence of magnitude, and of phoneme.

Kamikaze engine between wings;
to aim; kill off; reduce to nil; alone;
none; naught; cipher; the thing in nothing;
that guy on the couch in the empty home.

Frame-Drag

Flash-rapid blink, moments cut
into discrete bursts of light—
brief blossoms of line, mass, texture.

Predict this prophetic stutter,
falls that follow to flight—
broken blooms of being, unsure.

A silent film uppercut,
your day, evening, and night—
what's happening, happened, demure.

Eyeflow, your direction set
against what you want, but right—
what's behind, ahead, a mixture.

Jump cut, freefall, body/knife-whet
pulled, a fuse the moment ignites—
precess, reach ahead, cynosure.

Calques from Imaginary Languages

1.

The maskless eyelashes, painted sunflares
licking forehead cheekbone, corona
about gibbous optic organs, tears

seeing's fabric, black lacquer guitar
pickguards in bright spruce face, the Brahma's
dark pre-, pointing brain fingertips, lodestar

ocean reflection devoid, the Devil's hair
bun, flames with fuel hidden, deep trauma
orbiting cool orbs, behind where the stars

burn, send the light to find a way to find Allah.

2.

Lazy whores, hazy sky, the Lazarus
impulse to feed bulimic crypt cellars,
summer Hoseas in lousy Kansas

motel stairwells, horses' feedbags, calloused
lips nevertheless pull food, dwell where
tooth meets tongue, the zoo's gallus gallus

strut in confident black leather, ballast
over legs, bodybrain supports lamellar
armour, eggshell scripture, sweat glands, chalice

without rim, tense surface, water, wine, Kevlar.

3.

Gas can sutures screen door to trailer,
pickup flatbed flattened under suitcases
slid dovetail, each tight corner or failure

love makes, known firebrands, forsakes another
another and another in places
bioluminescent with terror's

torn truculence, tumid fascia, or fingers
hummocked, fingers' fingers, negative spaces
stitched, woven, embraced, pointed, gnarled ginger

root in lead paint, chrome, payload a veined lace.

The Ants

Strewn on the driveway, a spectacle—
neither swarm nor crowd, but an opera
gone still after a bomb separates the front
of house from the stage by way of what's between—
survivors stumbled about like straggled
scalpers calling out spares and outrageous asks,
stepping around what we no longer notice—
the lunch hour's sliver and shard, dog shit,
vagrant stones, tattered bodies of brood mates
crushed underfoot by absent passing above—
sopranos all, these tiny soldiers,
grunting under the ambitious weight of triage
carried home and pieced out amongst the hive
while dress shoes and penny loafers and patent
heels pass over and come down again—
touch the Earth as angels of destruction
on a wire, each footfall a kind of weather—

or

maybe just God's most accurate lightning.

Esau and I

(New Year's Day, 2009)

Esau and I trade birthright for lentils,
the red, red stuff of relative mourning; drunk
like water from shallow bowls, with coloured pills
on returning empty-handed from the hunt.

All my judgements are split these days, like twins
born racing to the light at mother's end;
poles with an earth caught between, fighting
their magnetic instinct to twist, but not bend.

The New Year starts with a red rocket sky,
revellers and wounded stumbling home;
halves of the planet divided by a line
over which fireworks bloom and missiles drone.

Drunk on wine and good cheer,
our countdowns descend to a chime.
The celebration still rings in our ears,
as dun tanks roll past the Armistice Line.

My brother and I have been separated
by worldview and age. Seeking to understand
our father's wishes, we build trust abetted
by the threat of common foes and common land.

Part of me is proud of what's been made here
since the banner of its bloody birth flew,
but another half, hung from my heel,
grapples with God before I can run him through.

Training Day

(September 2003)

In one hand, the paper with a photo of training
marines belly-down on the deck of a ship,
pointing black guns

out at an empty sea; in the other a mug of coffee
that's getting me through a half-read,
half-watched morning,

the first day of school laughing nervously across
the street. What are they aiming at out there
where nothing remains

still? From my sunroom it's impossible
to tell who will be what when
the evening breaks.

It would be nice to have such clear starts again.
Shooting the blue just to learn how
the gun stirs in your hands.

Innocent Bystanders

Two tables over, a couple argues
and we become tangled in their affair
the way bystanders get subdued
by a suicide bomber's need for prayer.

Sides are taken, parallels drawn, even
before we politely turn back to us,
a long-standing quarrel we imagined
long-solved keeping us here at cautious.

It seems like any break in this delicate
parity of well-arranged silence
could violate what we try to keep private
and take us beyond raucous glances.

Let's change tables and go back to solving
things in the hushed air of two like minds,
retreat from what's turning into a scene
and come here again at our own pace and time.

Toronto

On the street a man stands in the rain,
head down, holding a woman to his chest.
No, it's a black guitar case he holds, his arms
crossed over it. No, it is indeed a woman;

I can hear her weeping. The old white scar
on the back of my hand still gapes: a fish
hauled up by its cheek, the exposed
hook dipping into and out of flesh.

When the rain stops there's a slash of twilight
healing in the west, a spectacular
show of sun and filth where the buildings get low
and the highway opens up for a run.

I can't remember where I got this scar,
can you? It's knife straight, but away
from where a cut might happen by accident.
There's nothing I can do about it now.

Icarus in the Wax Museum

Imagine the boy inversed, real feathers
grafted to a wax body and winched
up near the museum's halogen ceiling;

cutting through climate-controlled weather,
starting to droop in the light, wrists pinched
with cable, wingtips eye-screwed and wheeling.

When he liquefies, dripping on those below,
his wings don't fly off, ascend on their own
to some girdered bliss, but instead remain

caught in The Fall; the body's soft tallow
drawn down, while its means of flight still drones
on through an honestly human rain.

(hubris isn't just about going up,
but what falls back down)

He can't reach Heaven but neither will he find Hell,
because we didn't just make his wings,
but the sun, the sky, and the man as well.

Rose

Surgery and injury kin, prune and plumb,
thorny trimmings piling up in the pot's
saucer, limbs stacked level to the grave's lip.

Cut and cut again, tree to bush to thumb
greened against those leaves unaware death's not
sensitive enough to know touch from grip.

Intake, sudden breath, beauty through pain's dumb
memory, the loss you know is a plot
compared to the wince you make with each snip.

Ligature (&)

At some point we blur and blend, make a shape of life,
stop defining the end of our skin by where
others begin, just the touch of two not enough.

I'm not sure I knew this when I first noticed those
conjugal conjunctions, phonemes bled to one,
marks in those spaces that seemed to want to say, *More.*

We crossed at *and*, at *et*, then began to mesh,
body and meaning, consecutive letters bent
from sound to grapheme to print strike to &.

Work, quiet symbols, what we wrap in on our selves,
an almost infinity, or infinity's
shape, almost. Two come one, struggling to stay bound.

State of Emergency

(September 2001 / January 2006)

1.

It's already snowed three feet when the newsman
approaches with his camera gear in tow,
looking for a degree of depth he can send
to the cables—the city's crumpled crow

knocked out on winter's frosted skyscraper,
men digging out cars, neighbours pitching in.
Strange comedy, this—part romance, part caper
—tragic and remote at times, but rich in

clownish annoyance. From the edge of my eye
he slides into view and holds out his mic
without the slightest word of civil invite—
a move that's my cue to stand and sigh, spike

the spade like Prospero's staff in the ashen
ice of the plough's latest pass at set design,
lean in wearily, smile in that sly fashion,
say—*It just keeps falling, but I'm doing fine.*

2.

Once I fled a burning shadow as it fell,
a poorly secured backdrop—aware each blink
could be the one that would extend, kill
the stage lights, let the darkness stretch out and drink

whatever strange draught my time was made of.
When the script said to run, I ran—helped those
I could, carried an old man up above
the dusty asphalt for a stretch—the twin snows

of shoes and foolscap-confetti falling
through a fog of crushed concrete, asbestos,
and disbelief. I sat for months mulling
that day's bizarre performance as best

I could—a silent and foreign Caliban,
jaw-clenched and stunned, unwilling to cajole
from my twisted brain some actor's acumen,
while others got applause for a smooth *Let's roll.*

3.

I can't tell from this frozen window whether
snow or ash, nature or nurture, will bury
us at the roadside—but any rough weather's
now a good enough excuse for worry.

When the wind changes, who's obliged to speak?
When the sky is falling, who must be informed?
It makes bad theatre, this love of *heartbreak*
—fact overacted, but underperformed.

Recite in the mic, a string of idle
words, three glass-eyed seconds of civic duty—
charmed, like Ariel's promise to make a bride
of Wonder for the arm of Chance, and be set free.

A bird flies into the camera lens,
the storm hammers down, buildings fall—life leaves
us each speechless for once—well rehearsed, cleansed,
island-bound on stage, not reciting, but live.

Whiteout

Pull the car over and take a moment
to note that this is where the road ends,
notwithstanding the memory of the path
continuing around the bend. The last
red taillights are painted over and the snow
presses its face up against the window,
begging to be let in. Turn the engine off,
it says, and hear this original soft
sound, a book of white nothing. I am life
without known rules: no signs, no lights, no lines
on the road; no ditches, asphalt, or curbs;
no people to see, no horizons or turns
to make; no destination. Draw aside.
Let your engine die and we'll compromise
temperature, colour, sound. I am life
where life heaves, turns and reads its final leaf.
Inside, the tick-tock of cooling machinery;
outside, the rattle ends this needless scenery.
If the road goes on without you, it goes blind.
Here, all is only static and knuckles cracking;
here you ease the tension ahead by waiting,
despite the chance of being hit from behind.

Cantus Firmus (Spring Morning)

Dear Lord, things are always already closing.
The sun is now over the hills and rising.
Daffs go ochre in the garden, crisping.
Age settles on the baby in teeth and talking.
The spider's presently pea-sized and growing.

A thought came to me through this accounting,
Subtle instance of near understanding.
A moment so sublime that in its writing
It disguised itself and hid in the waning
Beginning of this morning's latest ending.

Notes

Earlier versions of some of these poems first appeared in the following publications: *Alhambra Poetry Calendar* (Belgium), *Arts East* (Can), *Event* (Can), *Fiddlehead* (Can), *Granta* (UK), *Literary Review of Canada* (Can), *London Magazine* (UK), *The New Quarterly* (Can), *The New Welsh Review* (UK), *Riddle Fence* (Can), *Pasture* (NZ), *Pequod* (USA), and *The Walrus* (Can). Several poems from this book also appeared in *Exit Strategy*, a limited edition new-and-selected published by Kilmog Press of New Zealand.

The epigraph for "Brushfires" reads: ". . . *some skeletal remains initially thought to be single bodies were actually two people fused together by searing temperatures.*" — CNN, February 12, 2009

The epigraph for "State of Emergency": "*Be not afeard; the isle is full of noises, / Sounds and sweet airs, that give delight and hurt not.*" —*The Tempest, III:ii*

"Song for Memory" was adapted by The Once to a song for their album *Row Upon Row of the People They Know* (2011).

Many of these poems were written while working under grants from the Canada Council for the Arts, the Ontario Arts Council, and the Newfoundland and Labrador Arts Council.